DIGITAL AND INFORMATION LITERACY ™

SOCIAL
ACTIVISM ONLINE: GETTING INVOLVED

JOE GREEK

rosen publishing's
rosen central®

New York

Published in 2015 by The Rosen Publishing Group, Inc.
29 East 21st Street, New York, NY 10010

Copyright © 2015 by The Rosen Publishing Group, Inc.

First Edition

Library of Congress Cataloging-in-Publication Data

Greek, Joe.
Social activism online : getting involved/Joe Greek.
    pages cm—(Digital and information literacy)
Includes bibliographical references and index.
ISBN 978-1-4777-7655-1 (library bound)—ISBN 978-1-4777-7657-5 (pbk.)—ISBN 978-1-4777-7658-2 (6-pack)
1. Online social networks. I. Title.
HM742.G7394 2015
302.30285—dc23
                                                                2013051161

Manufactured in the United States of America

CONTENTS

INTRODUCTION

Accepting his high school's award for "Class Actor," New Jersey teen Jacob Rudolph began his speech by saying, "I've been acting every single day of my life." He continued, "You see me acting the part of straight Jacob, when I'm, in fact, an LGBT—lesbian, gay, bisexual, and transgender" (as quoted by *EDGE* Boston). During the speech, Jacob expressed his sympathy for students across the nation who feel as though they must keep their sexual identity a secret out of fear of being bullied or isolated. As he walked off the stage, the auditorium erupted in loud cheers of support.

In January 2013, Jacob's father uploaded a video of the speech to YouTube. The video, which has since been viewed more than 1.9 million times, quickly went viral and made it onto news channels. Almost overnight, Jacob had become an Internet sensation. He didn't let his fifteen minutes of Internet fame go to waste either. He decided to use the opportunity to call attention to a controversial form of "conversion therapy" that seeks to "turn" gays and lesbians into heterosexuals. The therapy is condemned by the American Psychiatric Association.

Using an online petition, Jacob set out to urge New Jersey governor Chris Christie to sign a bill into law that would ban the imposition of conversion therapy on minors. As was the case with the video, Jacob's petition

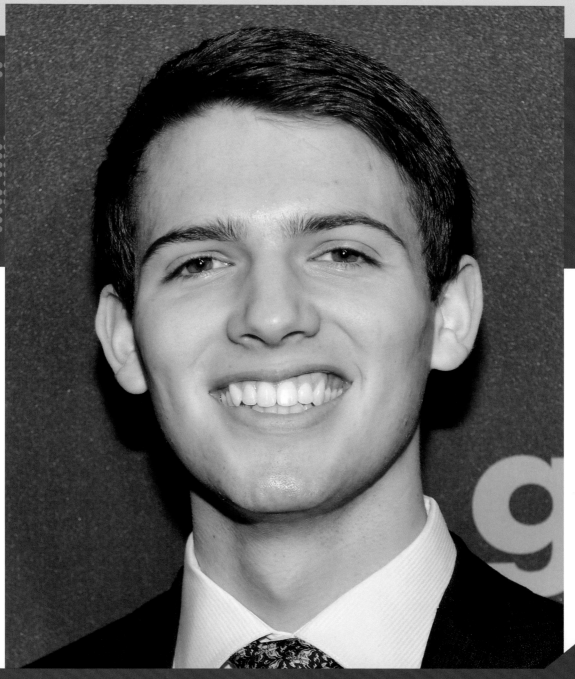

Jacob Rudolph's successful campaign to ban a controversial form of therapy in New Jersey began with an online petition that gained national attention.

quickly went viral and gained more than 140,000 signatures. Previously unknown to many people, conversion therapy suddenly became a highly discussed and debated topic among citizens and lawmakers in the state. On August 19, 2013, Christie signed a bill that officially made the practice of conversion therapy on individuals under eighteen years old illegal.

Jacob's story is just one of many successful tales of social activism in the digital age. People around the world are now using the web to create positive changes within their communities, countries, and abroad. In many ways, you have the world at your fingertips when you log onto the Internet, and you can use this unprecedented access and opportunity to change the world around you.

Chapter 1

Social Activism: From the Streets to the Web

he Internet has changed many aspects of the world we live in. From the way we communicate and receive and share information to the ways we build and maintain relationships, the Internet has forced much of the world to adapt to an online way of living. Even an activity like social activism, so associated in the popular mind with the streets and the "real world," has evolved to stay relevant and effective in the digital landscape.

How Social Activism Shapes the World

Flipping through the pages of your history textbook, you will discover example after example of social activism. In fact, much of the personal freedoms, civil liberties, and legal protections that we enjoy in present-day society can be traced back directly to the efforts of social activists.

The birth and emergence of the United States, for instance, is deeply rooted in social activism. Inhabitants of the original thirteen American

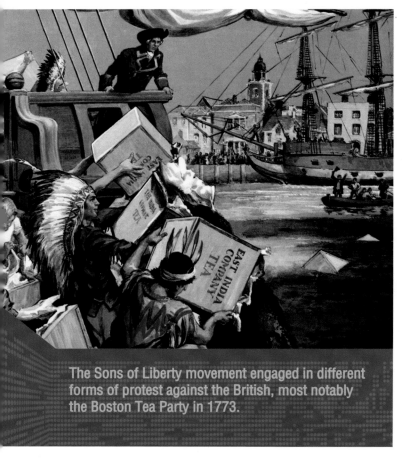

The Sons of Liberty movement engaged in different forms of protest against the British, most notably the Boston Tea Party in 1773.

colonies lacked elected representatives in the British Parliament. Yet they were still required to follow British laws and shoulder an increasingly heavy burden of taxation. When the British government passed the Stamp Act of 1765, which required the colonists to pay a tax on printed goods, the Sons of Liberty movement was born.

The efforts of the Sons of Liberty movement ranged from boycotting certain taxed goods, passing out antitax and anti-British pamphlets, and printing opinionated columns in newspapers to acts of intimidation against merchants who supported the British.

One of the most famous acts of protest carried out by the Sons of Liberty occurred on December 16, 1773, when activists threw a shipment of tea into Boston Harbor as an act of defiance against taxation on the product. Known as the Boston Tea Party, the event became a critical turning point in American history. Two years later, the colonies were at war with Great Britain, fighting to gain independence.

Ever since declaring independence from Great Britain in 1776, the United States—though still a young nation—was shaped by several transformative social activist movements. For example, the abolitionist movement of the 1830s to the 1870s helped bring an end to the enslavement of African

Americans. The success of the women's suffrage movement of the late nineteenth century and early twentieth century resulted in the creation of the Nineteenth Amendment, which guarantees women the right to vote. In 2008, the successes of these two movements could still be felt as voters in the Democratic presidential primary cast their ballots for either Hillary Clinton, future secretary of state and wife of former U.S. president Bill Clinton, or Barack Obama, a senator from Illinois. Obama went on to win the nomination and the ensuing presidential election to become the first African American president of the United States.

3:26 PM - 6 Nov 12 · Details   5h

Barack Obama @BarackObama
Four more years. pic.twitter.com/bAJE6Vom
▣ Hide photo   ← Reply ⇄ Retweet ★ Favorite

529,625   179,486
RETWEETS   FAVORITES   Flag media

People on Twitter and other social networks quickly engaged in conversation during Barack Obama's presidential victories in 2008 and 2012.

Early Signs of Online Activism

One of the earliest instances of online activism centered on the issue of privacy. In 1990, a time when, according to a United Nations Human Development Report, only eight out of every one thousand people in the United States used the Internet, the Lotus Development Corporation planned the release of a massive mailing list called *Lotus MarketPlace: Households*. The mailing list included the names of 120 million Americans and their personal information, including incomes, telephone numbers, addresses, and spending behaviors. The list was going to be made available on CDs, which could be purchased by the general public to view on their personal computers.

Computers and the web have made the ability to share, use, and even abuse personal information a common practice. The regulation of how businesses can handle customer information is frequently debated.

While this type of information had been frequently available to large marketing companies, *Households* made it possible for anyone off the street to obtain another individual's personal information without his or her consent. According to Mary J. Culnan, a member of Computer Professionals for Social Responsibility, public awareness of the issue skyrocketed after an article in the *Wall Street Journal* about *Households* was shown at computer industry conferences and then quickly spread nationwide via e-mail. As more people began to find out about *Households* through e-mail and discussion forums, Lotus soon received more than thirty thousand requests to be removed from the list. As a result of the unexpected public outcry, Lotus halted the production of *Households*. In the end, even in the years when very few people were able or interested enough to venture online, the Internet demonstrated its ability to inform and mobilize a large number of people who shared similar views about an issue and sought to adopt a common strategy of action.

The Web Before Facebook

Today, you can log on to your Facebook account from a smartphone and see what your family and friends are sharing with each other the very moment something gets posted. One of the most appealing aspects of social networks is how quick and easy it is to share your thoughts, pictures, videos, and other interesting things you find on the web or in the world around you with others. Over the past several years, social networks have become increasingly present in our daily lives. In a recent study by Experian Marketing Services, it was reported that the average American spent sixteen minutes per hour on social networks.

Yet even before Facebook and Twitter, the web was a social hive where individuals from across the globe could connect with one another. However, the web was not as accessible or as quick and easy to navigate as it is today. Up until the early 2000s, the majority of Internet connection speeds available to the public were vastly slower than they are currently. Mobile phones that could access the web didn't become available until

File   Edit   View   Favorites   Tools   Help

DOES ONLINE ACTIVISM EQUAL REAL-WORLD CHANGE?

Does Online Activism Equal Real-World Change?

Millions of American citizens took to the streets over the course of the civil rights movement of the 1950s and 1960s. As a result of the growing pressure exerted by their massive, organized protests and marches across the nation, Congress passed several laws that ended racial segregation and provided equal opportunities for individuals of all skin colors. Over the course of history, major changes to social problems, such as segregation, have required large numbers of people to become informed about current issues and take action to bring about change and progress.

In the Internet age, it is much easier for people to gather news and opinions on issues that shape the world around them. However, some argue that people can gain a false sense of accomplishment and active involvement in a social issue by signing online petitions and interacting on social networks alone. In an article on *Ars Technica*, American activist and former presidential nominee Ralph Nader, appearing at a speaking event at the University of California, is quoted as asking students in the audience, "Are big corporations afraid of the public use of the Internet? Does Congress fear the civic use of the Internet? Does the Pentagon fear the civic use of the Internet?" Nader then replied, "My tentative conclusion is that the Internet doesn't do a very good job of motivating action."

around 2007, when devices such as the iPhone were introduced and mobile phone reception improved dramatically.

Prior to the improvement of connection speeds, websites tended to be basic, focusing more on text rather than visual media, such as images and videos. Websites rich with visual media that you might commonly visit today, such as YouTube and Pinterest, would have taken several minutes to load on a computer using a dial-up connection. Nonetheless, as more people gained access to home computers in the late 1990s and early 2000s, the web became a revolutionary new platform with which to share information. Driving this spread of information, technologies such as e-mail, discussion boards, chat rooms, and instant messaging made it possible to quickly communicate with people whether they were in the next room or on the other side of the planet.

The Internet: Bringing Out the Masses

The U.S.-led war in Afghanistan that began in 2001 in the wake of the 9/11 terrorist attacks was a divisive topic during the early 2000s, both within the United States and abroad. The antiwar movement would reach unexpected levels in 2003 as discussions of another U.S.-led invasion, this time in Iraq, increased tensions around the world. Many people felt that President George W. Bush had not made a clear case for declaring war on Iraq. Still, his administration continued to speak strongly in favor of the necessity of putting troops on the ground.

After an antiwar protest in London, England, which was attended by upwards of four hundred thousand individuals, social movement groups began discussing the idea of organizing international protests. Activist websites such as MoveOn.org and TrueMajority.com became popular among supporters of the antiwar movement.

MoveOn, in particular, played a vital role in organizing individuals in the United States. After signing an online petition against a military strike in Iraq, individuals were sorted by state and could then contact each other to organize at local levels. Additionally, the organization began accepting donations online that were used for newspaper and television advertisements. The *New York Times* reported that the group was able to raise more than $300,000 within the first forty-eight hours. The average donation was

The web has been a powerful tool for organizations and protest groups to plan events. This 2007 Los Angeles demonstration against the war in Iraq was organized by MoveOn.org.

$30. In various countries, protests large and small occurred. Eventually, however, February 15, 2003, was agreed upon by antiwar protestors worldwide as a day of unified, international protests. Organizations and individuals across the planet quickly began organizing in preparation for a digital experiment in social activism that hadn't ever been performed at such a level.

Aside from traditional advertisements on radio stations, television channels, and newspapers, the web provided social activists with a new platform to organize and get the word out both offline and online. Keep in mind that organizing for social movements in the past generally required reaching out to people by phone, handing out fliers on the sidewalk, or going door to door. Now activists and organizations were able to reach out to others via online tools, such as e-mail and forums, to gain support and inform people of the times and locations of protests.

As February 15 drew closer, no one knew for certain how large turn-outs for the protests would be. The day did not disappoint. According to *Time* magazine, it's estimated that ten to fifteen million people filled the streets of more than six hundred cities across the planet. In Rome alone, more than three million protesters flooded the Italian capital. Outside of the United Nations headquarters in New York City, police commissioner Ray Kelly estimated that one hundred thousand people had attended the protest that stretched across twenty blocks.

To the dismay of the millions who had taken to the streets that day in solidarity, the United States ignored the mass global protests and invaded Iraq on March 19, 2003. Although the protesters were unable to claim a victory that day, they did manage to become part of one of the largest organized social activist efforts in history.

Chapter 2

Reborn: Social Activism in the Digital Age

Social activism has evolved over the past several decades in response to a world and populace that have become more connected than ever. The web has also produced new issues that have become important to society, such as the protection of online anonymity, security, and privacy. One of the more fascinating aspects of comparing social activism from the past to that of the present is that both still bring people together for a common cause. What has changed, though, are the methods that activists use to promote their causes.

Politics and Activism

In many ways, traditional politics and political activism have become things of the past. Politicians, activists, and the issues they care about have all found their places online. Politicians, for example, have increasingly used the Internet as a communication platform to reach voters. Through their campaign websites, politicians lay out their opinions on issues and how they

Political candidates and groups use the web to reach out to current and potential supporters. The grassroots organization Ready for Hillary launched its web campaign three years ahead of the 2016 U.S. presidential election.

intend to handle them if elected. Additionally, they can use their websites to attack opponents' voting records or personal backgrounds.

Rather than sending out physical mail that is costly and requires a lot of manpower, campaigns and political activist groups can now simply compile lists of e-mail addresses to send out updates, rally details, or contribution requests. Streaming video, which can be hosted on sites like YouTube, also makes it possible for politicians and activists to host live forums and debates that supporters everywhere can watch.

Door-to-Door No More: Online Petitions

Activists have also discovered that the web provides a new way to reach the public in order to gather signatures for petitions. Online petitions can be created using popular websites such as Change.org, which now has more than fifty-three million members. Activists can then share links to posted petitions via social networks, blogs, and e-mail. Supporters are able to sign the petition and share it with their online network of friends. The ease of signing and sharing an online petition makes it a popular tool for bringing attention to an issue. However, the legitimacy, impact, and ultimate effectiveness of online petitions have been frequently questioned. For example, comparable to traditional petitions, people have found ways to attach fake names to online

Online petitions are easy to create and share among supporters. However, their impact in the real world is often questioned.

petitions. Nonetheless, online petitions are becoming more difficult to cheat, while at the same time becoming increasingly popular.

Governments, including the United States, have also adopted online petitioning services that give citizens the opportunity to have their concerns heard by elected officials. For example, the White House launched its own petitioning system in 2011 called "We The People." Under this system, the White House will respond within thirty days to petitions that gather at least one hundred thousand signatures.

Following the 2012 school shooting at Sandy Hook Elementary in Newton, Connecticut, in which twenty students and six school employees were killed, a petition to increase gun control laws achieved the one hundred thousand mark within twenty-four hours. The Office of the President

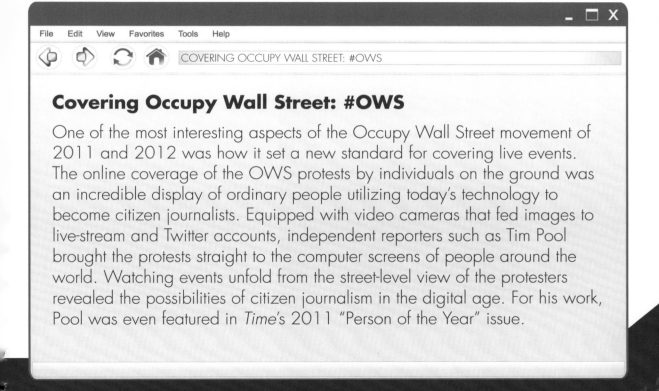

File   Edit   View   Favorites   Tools   Help

COVERING OCCUPY WALL STREET: #OWS

Covering Occupy Wall Street: #OWS

One of the most interesting aspects of the Occupy Wall Street movement of 2011 and 2012 was how it set a new standard for covering live events. The online coverage of the OWS protests by individuals on the ground was an incredible display of ordinary people utilizing today's technology to become citizen journalists. Equipped with video cameras that fed images to live-stream and Twitter accounts, independent reporters such as Tim Pool brought the protests straight to the computer screens of people around the world. Watching events unfold from the street-level view of the protesters revealed the possibilities of citizen journalism in the digital age. For his work, Pool was even featured in *Time*'s 2011 "Person of the Year" issue.

responded to the petition, as well as to thirty-two others related to gun control, stating that the White House would tackle the issue. Over the following months, Congress frequently debated gun control, and the issue also became a hot topic of conversation on social networks. Despite these actions, the U.S. government did not pass any significant gun control laws in the wake of the Sandy Hook massacre.

Organizing People with Hashtags

Activist organizations utilize the web to set up and promote events, such as meetings and protests. During the Arab Spring, a series of uprisings in the Middle East, people coordinated protests using Facebook and Twitter. By following discussions and trending topics on social networks, activists can get information and breaking news almost as soon as it happens. During the 2011 civil unrest in Egypt, for example, protesters tweeted about events that were unfolding in the streets. Using hashtags and phrases such as "#EgyptProtests," it was possible for the protesters to communicate with one another and gain a broader sense of what was happening in their country. How much of an actual role social networks play during social movements, such as the Arab Spring, is still difficult to measure.

The world was able to watch the 2011 Egyptian unrest unfold from the safety of home. Here, a protester uses Skype to stream a protest in Cairo's Tahrir Square.

Donations: The Online Bank

The web offers activists and organizations several ways to raise money for their causes. Websites and blogs, for example, can accept donations from a visitor by adding a PayPal button, which allows the contributor to transfer money digitally. Political fund-raising, in particular, has demonstrated in recent years how organizations are changing their approach to obtaining donations. According to a *Time* magazine article by Michael Scherer, the Obama presidential re-election campaign raised approximately $690 million digitally in 2012, which was close to $500 million more than was raised in his 2008 campaign. The 2012 campaign utilized several digital tools to accomplish this, including e-mail, social media, text messaging, and the Obama website.

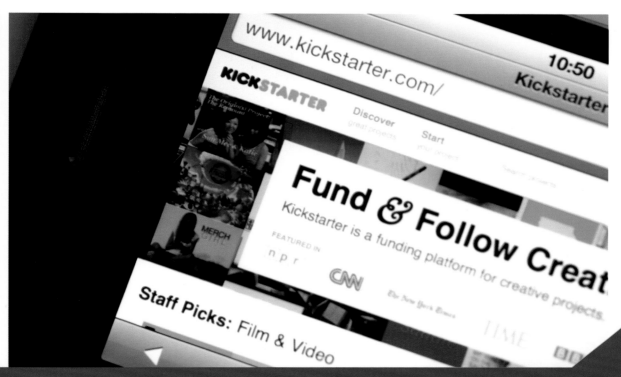

Crowdfunding sites, such as Kickstarter, allow users to pitch their ideas to online audiences in order to obtain funding for business, personal, or political use.

Crowdfunding sites have also become very popular for connecting with potential donors, investors, and venture capitalists (who provide cash for start-up businesses). These types of websites, such as Kickstarter, Crowdrise, and Razoo, enable groups to connect with individuals who might be willing to donate or lend money to a cause, individual, business, or idea that they value and in which they believe. There are hundreds of crowdfunding sites in existence that specialize in different interests. The way a crowdfunding campaign works varies from site to site. Users of Kickstarter, for example, set a financial goal and generally offer incentives (T-shirts, VIP tickets to an event, etc.) based on how much money an individual donates. These sites have funded numerous successful projects.

MYTHS & FACTS

MYTH If a petition gathers a certain number of signatures, the recipient or government will have to do what the petition asks.

FACT Even if five million people signed a petition that demanded a certain law to be passed, there are no laws that require the recipient to abide by its demands. However, a petition in many cases may bring attention to an issue that might have gone unnoticed otherwise and exert pressure on the recipient to act in accord with the petitioners' wishes.

MYTH Activists are hostile and confrontational.

FACT Activism is often associated with the word "protest," an activity that has a history of both peaceful engagement and hostile, or even violent, confrontation. Activism, however, is more than just protesting. Activists can engage in several activities besides protesting, including volunteer work, fund-raising, writing letters to elected officials, or walking door-to-door to raise awareness about an issue.

MYTH Activists simply want to avoid real work and instead hang out in the streets protesting everything associated with productive and law-abiding society.

FACT Activists are made up of people from all walks of life. For example, Mahatma Gandhi was a lawyer before he successfully led British-ruled India to independence by promoting nonviolent methods of protest.

Chapter 3

Online Activism Today

acebook founder Mark Zuckerberg announced in October 2012 that the iconic social network had reached a record-breaking milestone. More than eight years after its founding in 2004, Facebook had reached one billion members. In other words, out of the entire population of Earth, nearly one in seven people had a Facebook profile at the time of his announcement. With so many people accessing social networks such as Facebook and even more who browse the web on a daily basis, the opportunity to connect with your local community—and far beyond—is just one click away. Social networks can be great tools to keep in contact with friends and family, but they extend beyond connections with family and friends.

Charitable organizations, for example, are now turning to social networks to help raise money for their causes. In the aftermath of the devastating 2010 earthquake in Haiti, the Red Cross was able to raise $486 million in donations that was used for housing, medical supplies, clean water, and projects to help prepare Haitians for potential disasters in the future. According to *PRNews*, the Red Cross raised more than $32 million through

Survivors of the devastating 2010 earthquake in Haiti carry tarps, blankets, and hygiene kits given out by the Red Cross.

a text messaging campaign. It became widely publicized after a tweet calling for donations was shared more than 2.3 million times within forty-eight hours.

The success of the Red Cross campaign demonstrates how social networks can be used to spread a message that can create positive results. All around the world, people are using the web to organize, increase awareness, and raise money for the causes in which they believe. Even middle and high schoolers are using their social networking skills to create real change within their communities, nation, and even across the world.

Tweeting to Stomp Bullying

Bullying has always been a problem in schools. Many students have been victims or victimizers, and in some cases, both. According to data released by BullyingStatistics.org, nearly 2.7 million students are the victims of bullying every year. Because it occurs so frequently and affects so many, the issue of bullying has often become accepted as just a normal part of school life. However, the results of bullying, both in school and online, can result in serious consequences for the victims. They can suffer from depression and anxiety, and may even turn to self-harm as a way to cope with their pain.

In an effort to combat bullying and lift up his classmates when they might need it most, Iowa City teenager Jeremiah Anthony started a Twitter campaign

Bullies use the web as a tool to torment their victims. However, organizations such as Cyber Mentors are fighting back with online programs that tackle the issue and reach out to victims.

in 2011 that gained national attention. Using the handle @westhighbros, Jeremiah and his friends began sending messages to students at his school that pointed out their good qualities. "We just send compliments to people who we think are feeling bad a certain day or who have done something really good, like winning a state title," Jeremiah said in a video posted on HooplaHa.com. "I believe that showing the goodness in people is very integral to our account because so many people on Twitter and Facebook get cyberbullied because they're less than perfect."

Working within Twitter's 140-character limit, Jeremiah and his friends used the microblogging social network to promote a positive environment within their own school. Since 2011, their Twitter profile has sent out more than four thousand complimentary messages to fellow students, such as: "@mrachel080 your smile and charisma makes everyone else's day. School may be tough now but just keep doing your best and things will ease up!"

Students were not the only ones to be recognized for their positive qualities and contributions to the school. Even staff and administration were praised for their efforts, such as this tweet that recognized the school's janitors: "The custodial staff does so much for our school. They somehow get our huge school to look amazing every morning. Thank one of them tomorrow!"

Starting an anti-bullying campaign through Twitter or Facebook, such as Jeremiah and his friends did, is something that you can start within your own school. The great thing about his approach to the social issue of bullying is that it was free to start and the payoff was both huge and priceless. The @westhighbros effort is something that Jeremiah and his peers will be able to look back on with fond and very positive memories.

Disaster Aftermath: Raising Money for Those in Need

As spectators watched runners cross the finish line of the Boston Marathon on April 15, 2013, two bombs suddenly exploded with vicious force. In the aftermath of the devastation created by the bombs, three people were left

Mery Daniel *(center)* was one of the victims of the Boston Marathon bombing. Students at William Search Primary School in Weymouth, Massachusetts, raised more than $8,000 to cover her medical expenses.

dead and more than 170 were injured. Several of the victims were seriously injured and many lost limbs. While the horror of the events in Boston shook the nation, Florida teen Harris Stolzenberg decided that he could do something to help the victims.

Harris, seventeen, knew firsthand how traumatic it could be for a loved one to suffer emotionally and physically from the loss of a limb. Five years earlier, his younger brother Michael had contracted a serious skin infection that resulted in the loss of both legs and hands. Michael was fortunate enough to receive prosthetic legs that allowed him to return to a normal life among his peers. His new legs worked so well, in fact, that he was able to compete against his friends in football and lacrosse. Realizing how expensive prosthetic limbs could be, Harris knew that several of the Boston victims

File   Edit   View   Favorites   Tools   Help

BLOGGING AGAINST THE TALIBAN

Blogging Against the Taliban

Malala Yousafzai, a teenager from rural Pakistan, earned international recognition for courageously speaking out against the strict, political organization known as the Taliban. Using a fake name, Yousafzai began blogging for the BBC about the difficulties of living under Taliban rule, and in particular, the Taliban's fight against girls attending school. Only eleven years old when she began blogging, she became a hero in the women's right to education movement after her identity was revealed. At the same time, however, the Taliban branded her an enemy.

On October 9, 2012, Yousafzai was shot twice by a Taliban supporter as she rode the bus home from school. Miraculously, she managed to recover from her injuries after receiving medical treatment and rehabilitation in England. Even after the attempt on her life, Yousafzai continues to speak out against the Taliban. Her story, which began with a series of blog posts, has inspired many young girls across the world. In April 2013, *Time* magazine included Yousafzai as one of its "100 Most Influential People in the World."

Malala Yousafzai addresses the European Parliament in 2013 after being awarded the Sakharov human rights prize for speaking against the Taliban's refusal to allow all children a right to an education.

would most likely need financial help to afford the devices—a luxury many people are unable to pay for.

Harris came up with the idea to run the 2014 Boston Marathon in support of the victims and to raise money that would then be donated to them. With the goal of raising $1 million before the marathon, Harris enlisted the help of friends to build a website for his cause that people could donate money through. The campaign, called Mikey's Run, went viral after Harris posted pictures of his brother on the social photo-sharing site Imgur. The captions explained his intention to raise money for the marathon victims. Additionally, Harris used Facebook and Twitter to raise awareness about Mikey's Run. Soon the campaign was picked up by major news outlets and donations poured in.

By November 2013, Mikey's Run had raised more than $200,000 for the victims through PayPal, which is a service that allows people to transfer money to one another online. Even if the campaign did not reach his original goal of $1 million, Harris's selfless actions would help many people in need of assistance and bring light to the suffering of amputees. The outpouring of goodwill from complete strangers has even inspired Harris to consider working beyond the 2014 Boston Marathon to help amputees. "The goal, if this gets big enough, is not to stop at the Boston Marathon," Harris told *USA Today*. "We can expand to help other amputees who don't get the recognition and help they need. This could form into a [nonprofit] down the road and help a lot of other people."

Girls Banding Together

Walking door-to-door to obtain signatures on a petition was once a very popular way to gather support for a cause. People still occasionally will knock on your door to ask for donations or signatures, but the web has greatly impacted this method of activism. Websites such as Change.org and iPetitions.org have removed much of the physical work that was once needed to get signatures. The ease of sharing a link through an online petition—and the fact that most of the websites that provide such services are free—has made them very popular among activists.

From left to right, teenagers Emma Stydahar, Julia Bluhm, and Natasha Williams protest against *Seventeen* magazine outside of the publication's headquarters in New York City.

Online petitions, however, can be used to empower a variety of social activism movements and create beneficial discussions on important issues. At fourteen years old, Julia Bluhm was well aware that the type of models that fashion magazines, such as *Seventeen*, choose to print could negatively impact a girl's body image. Many models who appear in ads or on the runway are often very thin or underweight. Young girls can sometimes develop self-esteem issues or eating disorders because they may feel they don't measure up to the supposedly ideal body type that appears in fashion magazines.

Bluhm believed that *Seventeen*, in particular, had become a contributing force to this problem. "I've always just known how Photoshop can have a big effect on girls and their body image and how they feel about themselves," Bluhm told the *Huffington Post*. "You need to see something realistic—you need to see a reflection of what truly represents a teenage girl nowadays."

Using Change.org, Bluhm started a petition to get *Seventeen* to "commit to printing one unaltered—real—photo spread per month." The petition became very popular and picked up speed on social networks such as Twitter and Facebook. By the time Bluhm and a group of girls delivered the petition to the magazine's headquarters in New York City, eighty-four thousand people had signed their support. Ann Shoket, the magazine's editor-in-chief, responded positively to Bluhm and the supporters' petition. In a letter from the editor published in the August 2012 issue of the magazine, Shoket announced that the staff had made a pact to "never change girls' body or face shapes" and include only images of "real girls and models that are healthy."

Chapter 4

Now It's Your Turn!

Feeling passionate about a social issue is only the first step to becoming an activist. Taking that passion and doing something with it is the next step. With your knowledge of the web and social networks, you can become involved with social movements to help create a better world.

Start Building Your Network

In a May 1963 speech in Birmingham, Alabama, civil rights leader Dr. Martin Luther King Jr. said, "There is power in unity and there is power in numbers." True to Dr. King's message, it is certainly more difficult for one person to change society without the support of others. That said, you can use the web to seek out and connect with people and groups. The following are just a few examples of how you can begin to network:

- Join or create a discussion forum: Use a search engine to seek out forums that are based on your interests. Reddit.com, for example, features several activist discussion boards and allows you to create your own.
- Facebook groups: Use Facebook's search feature to find and join groups dedicated to your social cause.
- Find offline events: With a parent or guardian, use Facebook or activist websites to find local events that you can attend. Meeting experienced activists offline is a great way to learn more about your cause and how you can help.

Students can use the web to access a variety of tools that are used by modern social movements. Finding and connecting with other movement supporters is often a click away.

Create Your Own Digital Content

There's no better time than now to begin forming and recording your own opinions on social issues. Uploading your thoughts online, however, should be approached with much caution. How you feel today about a particular subject may not necessarily remain the same in the years ahead. It's important to understand that it is extremely difficult to permanently remove anything from the Internet. Pictures or blog posts that you deleted, for example, may be saved and hosted on sites such as Internet Archive. Before you upload material online, be sure to let an adult review it so that he or she can give you helpful advice.

File   Edit   View   Favorites   Tools   Help

ONLINE ACTIVISM AS A CAREER?

Online Activism as a Career?

If social activism is your passion in life, you can turn that passion into a career. There are thousands of organizations dedicated to numerous social causes. Many of these organizations rely on trained staff to run their offline and online operations. Web engineers who specialize in creating and maintaining websites are in high demand in many career fields. With the popularity of social networks, activist organizations and nonprofit, issue-oriented groups are increasingly relying on experienced social networkers to promote and monitor all developments relating to their cause. Career-oriented activism websites, such as ActivistJobBoard.com, offer useful information, tips, and resources that will help you gain a better knowledge of how you can put your digital skills to work.

Blogging is an easy way to begin writing about a social cause that you care about. Free blogging services, such as Wordpress.org and Blogger.com, provide easy-to-use tools and guides to help you get started. When you've created a blog post, you can then share it with your social network or activist group.

Additionally, you can create videos where you discuss your social cause. You can make your own quality videos using a web cam or smartphone. Easy-to-use video editing programs, such as iMovie, also allow you to give your videos a polished look. Once you've made a video, you can upload it to YouTube and then share it with your networks.

Voicing an opinion is not the same as being heard. Using the web to share thoughts is one way to start an online conversation with those who might support your movement.

Your Opinion Counts: Be Heard!

You have a voice that matters. For change to happen, it often requires people to speak up and be heard by others. There are many ways that you can use the web to contact the people who have the power and authority to make the change you want to see happen. The online petition, for example, is an excellent tool for raising awareness. Once you've collected a sizable number of signatures, you can then deliver it to an elected representative, individual, or group that can correct what you feel is wrong or implement a policy or program that you feel is important.

Writing directly to someone is also a great way to send your message. The website of a politician or organization that you may want to contact will

Today's social activists have the knowledge and ability to use both online and offline methods to bring about change in their own communities and lives.

usually have an e-mail address located at the bottom of the site or on a contact page. When writing to someone, be sure to be polite because they may ignore hateful or angry messages.

Open letters, which were traditionally printed in newspapers, are public messages that are directed to an individual or group. They are intended to raise awareness and often call for action from the public. Now you can send an open letter to a newspaper's website or to popular blogs. If you create a well-written message, the editor may post it online for all readers to see.

There are many ways you can become an activist and seek to promote positive change in society. Often, change can begin within your community, and then it can spread throughout the world. All it takes is dedication, patience, and heart.

TEN GREAT QUESTIONS

TO ASK A VETERAN ACTIVIST

1   What type of social problems have you worked on?

2   Why do you think these problems exist?

3   What sort of approaches did you use to address them?

4   Were your efforts ever successful, and how does an activist define success?

5   What seems to be the most successful way to raise awareness?

6   Do you need any special skills for your work?

7   Do you think the Internet has been good for activism?

8   How have you used the Internet as an activist?

9   What do you like most and least about being an activist?

10   What advice do you wish you could give your younger self?

GLOSSARY

adapt To change in order to survive or work better in a new environment.

anonymity The state of being unknown to others.

boycott A refusal to purchase goods or do business with an individual, organization, or country as an act of protest.

forum A meeting place or website where discussions on a topic are held.

hashtag A word or phrase that is set behind a pound sign (#) and is used on the Internet to mark discussions on certain topics.

live-stream To transmit live video across the Internet to an individual or audience.

milestone A significant point that is reached by an individual or organization that marks an important change.

Parliament The legislative branch of the British government; more generally, a legislative, or law-making, governmental body.

prosthetic limb An artificial device used to replace an arm or leg that someone may have lost because of an injury or birth defect.

rehabilitation Treatment that is used to help an individual recover from an injury or illness.

representative A person who is elected or appointed to speak on behalf of others.

scam The use of dishonesty or false promises to obtain money from someone.

segregation The act of setting an individual or group of people apart from others based on their skin color or other differences.

suffrage The right of an individual or group to vote in political elections.

unaltered Not edited or changed in any way.

viral When an image, video, website, or other form of online media becomes popular due to being rapidly shared on the Internet by thousands or even millions of users.

Amnesty International
5 Penn Plaza
New York, NY 10010
(212) 807-8400
Website: http://www.amnestyinternational.org
Amnesty International is the world's largest grassroots organization devoted
    to raising awareness of, investigating, and exposing human rights
    violations around the world.

Egale Canada Human Rights Trust (ECHRT)
185 Carlton Street
Toronto, ON M5A 2K7
Canada
(416) 964-7887
Website: http://www.egale.ca
The ECHRT advocates for the protection and equal rights of Canada's LGBT
    community and family members through education and awareness
    campaigns.

Habitat for Humanity
121 Habitat Street
Americus, GA 31709-3498
(229) 924-6935
Website: http://www.habitat.org
Habitat for Humanity is an international organization that relies on a network
    of volunteers and donors to build and repair houses for individuals and
    families in need of affordable housing.

National Organization for Women (NOW)
1100 H Street NW, Suite 300
Washington, DC 20005
(202) 628-8669
Website: http://www.now.org
NOW is the largest organization in the United States that is dedicated to
    fighting for the equality of all women in the workplace, schools, justice
    system, and in society as a whole.

Your Life Counts
Suite GG5B, Seaway Mall
800 Niagara Street North
Welland, ON L3C 5Z4
Canada
(905) 321-2771
Website: http://www.yourlifecounts.org
Through education, community outreach, and online support, Your Life
    Counts seeks to help young people and families avoid self-destructive
    behaviors than can lead to suicide.

Websites

Due to the changing nature of Internet links, Rosen Publishing has developed an online list of websites related to the subject of this book. This site is updated regularly. Please use this link to access the list:

http://www.rosenlinks.com/DIL/activ

FOR FURTHER READING

Ferguson Publishing. *Activism* (Ferguson's Careers in Focus). New York, NY: Ferguson Publishing, 2011.

Halpin, Mikki. *It's Your World—If You Don't Like It, Change It: Activism for Teenagers*. New York, NY: Simon Pulse, 2008.

Hamilton, Jill. *Activism* (Issues That Concern You). Farmington, MI: Greenhaven Press, 2009.

Hunter, Zach. *Generation Change: Roll Up Your Sleeves and Change the World*. New York, NY: HarperCollins, 2009.

Levinson, Cynthia. *We've Got a Job: The 1963 Birmingham Children's March*. Atlanta, GA: Peachtree Publishers, 2012.

Lewis, Barbara A. *The Teen Guide to Global Action: How to Connect with Others* (Near & Far) to Create Social Change. Minneapolis, MN: Free Spirit Publishing, 2007.

Marsico, Katie. *Women's Right to Vote: America's Suffrage Movement*. Buffalo, NY: Marshall Cavendish, 2010.

McGinty, Alice B. *Gandhi: A March to the Sea*. Seattle, WA: Two Lions, 2013.

National Geographic. *Every Human Has Rights: What You Need to Know About Your Human Rights*. Des Moines, IA: National Geographic Children's Books, 2008.

Rappaport, Doreen. *Martin's Big Words: The Life of Dr. Martin Luther King, Jr.* Rev. ed. New York, NY: Hyperion Book, 2007.

Weinick, Suzanne. *Understanding Your Rights in the Information Age* (Personal Freedom & Civic Duty). New York, NY: Rosen Publishing, 2013.

BIBLIOGRAPHY

Amand, Jason St. "NJ Teen Activist Launches Campaign Against Conversion Therapy." *Edge*, March 1, 2013. Retrieved November 2013 (http://www.edgeboston.com/?142118).

Culnan, Mary J. "The Lessons of the Lotus MarketPlace: Implications for Consumer Privacy in the 1990s." Computer Professionals for Social Responsibility, 1991. Retrieved November 2013 (http://cpsr.org/prevsite/conferences/cfp91/culnan.html).

Dartnell, Michael Y. *Insurgency Online: Web Activism and Global Conflict.* Toronto, ON, Canada: University of Toronto Press, 2006.

Gerbaudo, Paolo. *Tweets and the Streets: Social Media and Contemporary Activism.* New York, NY: Pluto Press, 2012.

Hands, Joss. *@ Is For Activism: Dissent, Resistance, and Rebellion in a Digital Culture.* New York, NY: Pluto Press, 2011.

Haughney, Christine. "*Seventeen* Magazine Vows to Show Girls 'as They Really Are.'" *New York Times*, July 3, 2012. Retrieved November 2013 (http://mediadecoder.blogs.nytimes.com/2012/07/03/after-petition-drive-seventeen-magazine-commits-to-show-girls-as-they-really-are).

Kim, Eun Kyung. "Teen Uses Tweets to Compliment His Classmates." *Today*, January 8, 2013. Retrieved November 2013 (http://www.today.com/news/teen-uses-tweets-compliment-his-classmates-1B7882246).

Lasar, Matthew. "Ralph Nader: Internet Not So Hot at 'Motivating Action.'" *Ars Technica*, 2009. Retrieved November 2013 (http://arstechnica.com/tech-policy/2009/05/ralph-nader-internet-not-so-hot-at-motivating-action).

Litman, Laken. "Teens Hope to Raise $1 Million for Boston Marathon Amputees." *USA Today*, April 24, 2013. Retrieved November 2013 (http://ftw.usatoday.com/2013/04/brothers-raise-money-for-boston-marathon-amputees).

Manjoo, Farhad. "Online Giving, One Person at a Time." *New York Times*, November 10, 2010. Retrieved November 2013 (http://www.nytimes.com/2010/11/11/giving/11SOCIAL.html?pagewanted=all&_r=0).

McCaughey, Martha, and Michael D. Ayers, eds. *Cyberactivism: Online Activism in Theory and Practice*. New York, NY: Routledge, 2003.

Milan, Stefania. *Social Movements and Their Technologies: Wiring Social Change*. New York, NY: Palgrave Macmillan, 2013.

Miller, Claire Cain. "How Obama's Internet Campaign Changed Politics." *New York Times*, November 7, 2008. Retrieved November 2013 (http://bits.blogs.nytimes.com/2008/11/07/how-obamas-internet-campaign-changed-politics).

Pickerill, Jenny. *Cyberprotest: Environmental Activism Online*. Manchester, England: Manchester University Press, 2010.

United Nations Regional Information Center for Western Europe. "Malala Yousafzai Receives the Sakharov Prize 2013." November 20, 2013. Retrieved November 2013 (http://www.unric.org/en/latest-un-buzz/28855-malala-yousafzai-receives-the-sakharov-prize-2013).

INDEX

P

PayPal, 21, 30
political activism, 16–20
political campaigns, 16, 17, 21, 22
privacy, 10–11
protests, 12, 13–15, 19, 20, 23

R

Red Cross, 24–25
Reddit.com, 34

S

Seventeen (magazine), 31–32
smartphones, 11–12
social activism
    careers in, 35
    history of, 7–9
    myths and facts, 23
    online activism (early signs), 10–11
    and politics, 16–17
    protests, 12, 13–15, 19, 20, 23

Sons of Liberty, 8
suffrage movement, 9

T

Taliban, 29
terrorism, 13, 27–28
TrueMajority.com, 13
Twitter, 19, 20, 26, 27, 30, 32

W

Web engineers, 35
"We The People" (petitioning system), 19
Wordpress.org, 36

Y

Yousafzai, Malala, 29
YouTube, 17, 36

Z

Zuckerberg, Mark, 24

About the Author

Growing up in rural Tennessee, Joe Greek eventually found his way to New York City, where he worked for online publications and at a publishing company. With a background in journalism, he has written primarily on the topics of technology, social media, and small business. When he is able to take a break from typing up a story, he enjoys volunteering with local organizations that feed the less fortunate.

Photo Credits

Cover and p. 1 (left) © iStockphoto.com/Nicolae Socaciu, (center left) © iStockphoto.com/ersler, (center right, right) © iStockphoto.com/hocus-focus; p. 5 Larry Busacca/Getty Images; p. 8 The Bridgeman Art Library/Getty Images; p. 9 Gabriel Bouys/AFP/Getty Images; p. 10 LuminaStock/E+/Getty Images; p. 14 David McNew/Getty Images; p. 17 Karen Bleier/AFP/Getty Images; p. 18 sturti/E+/Getty Images; p. 20 Mohammed Abed/AFP/Getty Images; p. 21 © iStockphoto.com/SeanShot; pp. 25, 28, 31 © AP Images; p. 26 Press Association/AP Images; p. 29 Patrick Hertzog/AFP/Getty Images; p. 34 Dean Mitchell/iStock/Thinkstock; p. 36 Chris Schmidt/E+/Getty Images; p. 37 Yellow Dog Productions/Photodisc/Getty Images; cover (background) and interior page graphics © iStockphoto.com/suprun

Designer: Nicole Russo; Photo Researcher: Karen Huang